WTF
IS MY
PASSWORD

NO MORE BRAIN FARTS TRYING TO REMEMBER THE SHIT PASSWORDS

I0021386

Date:_____

Website:_____

Username:_____

Password:_____

Notes:_____

_____

_____

Date:_____

Website:_____

Username:_____

Password:_____

Notes:_____

_____

_____

Date:_____

Website:_____

Username:_____

Password:_____

Notes:_____

_____

_____

Date:_____

Website:_____

Username:_____

Password:_____

Notes:_____

_____

_____

Date:_____

Website:_____

Username:_____

Password:_____

Notes:_____

_____

_____

Date:_____

Website:_____

Username:_____

Password:_____

Notes:_____

_____

_____

Date:_____

Website:_____

Username:_____

Password:_____

Notes:_____

_____

_____

Date:_____

Website:_____

Username:_____

Password:_____

Notes:_____

_____

_____

Date:_____

Website:_____

Username:_____

Password:_____

Notes:_____

_____

_____

Date:_____

Website:_____

Username:_____

Password:_____

Notes:_____

_____

_____

Date:_____

Website:_____

Username:_____

Password:_____

Notes:_____

_____

_____

Date:_____

Website:_____

Username:_____

Password:_____

Notes:_____

_____

_____

Date:_____

Website:_____

Username:_____

Password:_____

Notes:_____

_____

_____

Date:_____

Website:_____

Username:_____

Password:_____

Notes:_____

_____

_____

Date:_____

Website:_____

Username:_____

Password:_____

Notes:_____

_____

_____

Date:_____

Website:_____

Username:_____

Password:_____

Notes:_____

_____

_____

Date:_____

Website:_____

Username:_____

Password:_____

Notes:_____

_____

_____

Date:_____

Website:_____

Username:_____

Password:_____

Notes:_____

_____

_____

Date:_____

Website:_____

Username:_____

Password:_____

Notes:_____

_____

_____

Date:_____

Website:_____

Username:_____

Password:_____

Notes:_____

_____

_____

Date:_____

Website:_____

Username:_____

Password:_____

Notes:_____

_____

_____

Date:_____

Website:_____

Username:_____

Password:_____

Notes:_____

_____

_____

Date:_____

Website:_____

Username:_____

Password:_____

Notes:_____

_____

_____

Date:_____

Website:_____

Username:_____

Password:_____

Notes:_____

_____

_____

Date:_____

Website:_____

Username:_____

Password:_____

Notes:_____

_____

_____

Date:_____

Website:_____

Username:_____

Password:_____

Notes:_____

_____

_____

Date:_____

Website:_____

Username:_____

Password:_____

Notes:_____

_____

_____

Date:_____

Website:_____

Username:_____

Password:_____

Notes:_____

_____

_____

Date:_____

Website:_____

Username:_____

Password:_____

Notes:_____

_____

_____

Date:_____

Website:_____

Username:_____

Password:_____

Notes:_____

_____

_____

Date:_____

Website:_____

Username:_____

Password:_____

Notes:_____

_____

_____

Date:_____

Website:_____

Username:_____

Password:_____

Notes:_____

_____

_____

Date:_____

Website:_____

Username:_____

Password:_____

Notes:_____

_____

_____

Date:_____

Website:_____

Username:_____

Password:_____

Notes:_____

_____

_____

Date:_____

Website:_____

Username:_____

Password:_____

Notes:_____

_____

_____

Date:_____

Website:_____

Username:_____

Password:_____

Notes:_____

_____

_____

Date:_____

Website:_____

Username:_____

Password:_____

Notes:_____

_____

_____

Date:_____

Website:_____

Username:_____

Password:_____

Notes:_____

_____

_____

Date:_____

Website:_____

Username:_____

Password:_____

Notes:_____

_____

_____

Date:_____

Website:_____

Username:_____

Password:_____

Notes:_____

_____

_____

Date:_____

Website:_____

Username:_____

Password:_____

Notes:_____

_____

_____

Date:_____

Website:_____

Username:_____

Password:_____

Notes:_____

_____

_____

Date:_____

Website:_____

Username:_____

Password:_____

Notes:_____

_____

_____

Date:_____

Website:_____

Username:_____

Password:_____

Notes:_____

_____

_____

Date:_____

Website:_____

Username:_____

Password:_____

Notes:_____

_____

_____

Date:_____

Website:_____

Username:_____

Password:_____

Notes:_____

_____

_____

Date:_____

Website:_____

Username:_____

Password:_____

Notes:_____

_____

_____

Date:_____

Website:_____

Username:_____

Password:_____

Notes:_____

_____

_____

Date:_____

Website:_____

Username:_____

Password:_____

Notes:_____

_____

_____

Date:_____

Website:_____

Username:_____

Password:_____

Notes:_____

_____

_____

Date:_____

Website:_____

Username:_____

Password:_____

Notes:_____

_____

_____

Date:_____

Website:_____

Username:_____

Password:_____

Notes:_____

_____

_____

Date:_____

Website:_____

Username:_____

Password:_____

Notes:_____

_____

_____

Date:_____

Website:_____

Username:_____

Password:_____

Notes:_____

_____

_____

Date:_____

Website:_____

Username:_____

Password:_____

Notes:_____

_____

_____

Date:_____

Website:_____

Username:_____

Password:_____

Notes:_____

_____

_____

Date:_____

Website:_____

Username:_____

Password:_____

Notes:_____

_____

_____

Date:_____

Website:_____

Username:_____

Password:_____

Notes:_____

_____

_____

Date:_____

Website:_____

Username:_____

Password:_____

Notes:_____

_____

_____

Date:_____

Website:_____

Username:_____

Password:_____

Notes:_____

_____

_____

Date:_____

Website:_____

Username:_____

Password:_____

Notes:_____

_____

_____

Date:_____

Website:_____

Username:_____

Password:_____

Notes:_____

_____

_____

Date:_____

Website:_____

Username:_____

Password:_____

Notes:_____

_____

_____

Date:_____

Website:_____

Username:_____

Password:_____

Notes:_____

_____

_____

Date:_____

Website:_____

Username:_____

Password:_____

Notes:_____

_____

_____

Date:_____

Website:_____

Username:_____

Password:_____

Notes:_____

_____

_____

Date:_____

Website:_____

Username:_____

Password:_____

Notes:_____

_____

_____

Date:_____

Website:_____

Username:_____

Password:_____

Notes:_____

_____

_____

Date:_____

Website:_____

Username:_____

Password:_____

Notes:_____

_____

_____

Date:_____

Website:_____

Username:_____

Password:_____

Notes:_____

_____

_____

Date:_____

Website:_____

Username:_____

Password:_____

Notes:_____

_____

_____

Date:_____

Website:_____

Username:_____

Password:_____

Notes:_____

_____

_____

Date:_____

Website:_____

Username:_____

Password:_____

Notes:_____

_____

_____

Date:_____

Website:_____

Username:_____

Password:_____

Notes:_____

_____

_____

Date:_____

Website:_____

Username:_____

Password:_____

Notes:_____

_____

_____

Date:_____

Website:_____

Username:_____

Password:_____

Notes:_____

_____

_____

Date:_____

Website:_____

Username:_____

Password:_____

Notes:_____

_____

_____

Date:_____

Website:_____

Username:_____

Password:_____

Notes:_____

_____

_____

Date:_____

Website:_____

Username:_____

Password:_____

Notes:_____

_____

_____

Date:_____

Website:_____

Username:_____

Password:_____

Notes:_____

_____

_____

Date:_____

Website:_____

Username:_____

Password:_____

Notes:_____

_____

_____

Date:_____

Website:_____

Username:_____

Password:_____

Notes:_____

_____

_____

Date:_____

Website:_____

Username:_____

Password:_____

Notes:_____

_____

_____

Date:_____

Website:_____

Username:_____

Password:_____

Notes:_____

_____

_____

Date:_____

Website:_____

Username:_____

Password:_____

Notes:_____

_____

_____

Date:_____

Website:_____

Username:_____

Password:_____

Notes:_____

_____

_____

Date:_____

Website:_____

Username:_____

Password:_____

Notes:_____

_____

_____

Date:_____

Website:_____

Username:_____

Password:_____

Notes:_____

_____

_____

Date:_____

Website:_____

Username:_____

Password:_____

Notes:_____

_____

_____

Date:_____

Website:_____

Username:_____

Password:_____

Notes:_____

_____

_____

Date:_____

Website:_____

Username:_____

Password:_____

Notes:_____

_____

_____

Date:_____

Website:_____

Username:_____

Password:_____

Notes:_____

_____

_____

Date:_____

Website:_____

Username:_____

Password:_____

Notes:_____

_____

_____

Date:_____

Website:_____

Username:_____

Password:_____

Notes:_____

_____

_____

Date:_____

Website:_____

Username:_____

Password:_____

Notes:_____

_____

_____

Date:_____

Website:_____

Username:_____

Password:_____

Notes:_____

_____

_____

Date:_____

Website:_____

Username:_____

Password:_____

Notes:_____

_____

_____

Date:_____

Website:_____

Username:_____

Password:_____

Notes:_____

_____

_____

Date:_____

Website:_____

Username:_____

Password:_____

Notes:_____

_____

_____

Date:_____

Website:_____

Username:_____

Password:_____

Notes:_____

_____

_____

Date:_____

Website:_____

Username:_____

Password:_____

Notes:_____

_____

_____

Date:_____

Website:_____

Username:_____

Password:_____

Notes:_____

_____

_____

Date:_____

Website:_____

Username:_____

Password:_____

Notes:_____

_____

_____

Date:_____

Website:_____

Username:_____

Password:_____

Notes:_____

_____

_____

Date:_____

Website:_____

Username:_____

Password:_____

Notes:_____

_____

_____

Date:_____

Website:_____

Username:_____

Password:_____

Notes:_____

_____

_____

Date:_____

Website:_____

Username:_____

Password:_____

Notes:_____

_____

_____

Date:_____

Website:_____

Username:_____

Password:_____

Notes:_____

_____

_____

Date:_____

Website:_____

Username:_____

Password:_____

Notes:_____

_____

_____

Date:_____

Website:_____

Username:_____

Password:_____

Notes:_____

_____

_____

Date:_____

Website:_____

Username:_____

Password:_____

Notes:_____

_____

_____

Date:_____

Website:_____

Username:_____

Password:_____

Notes:_____

_____

_____

Date:_____

Website:_____

Username:_____

Password:_____

Notes:_____

_____

_____

Date:_____

Website:_____

Username:_____

Password:_____

Notes:_____

_____

_____

Date:_____

Website:_____

Username:_____

Password:_____

Notes:_____

_____

_____

Date:_____

Website:_____

Username:_____

Password:_____

Notes:_____

_____

_____

Date:_____

Website:_____

Username:_____

Password:_____

Notes:_____

_____

_____

Date:_____

Website:_____

Username:_____

Password:_____

Notes:_____

_____

_____

Date:_____

Website:_____

Username:_____

Password:_____

Notes:_____

_____

_____

Date:_____

Website:_____

Username:_____

Password:_____

Notes:_____

_____

_____

Date:_____

Website:_____

Username:_____

Password:_____

Notes:_____

_____

_____

Date:_____

Website:_____

Username:_____

Password:_____

Notes:_____

_____

_____

Date:_____

Website:_____

Username:_____

Password:_____

Notes:_____

_____

_____

Date:_____

Website:_____

Username:_____

Password:_____

Notes:_____

_____

_____

Date:_____

Website:_____

Username:_____

Password:_____

Notes:_____

_____

_____

Date:_____

Website:_____

Username:_____

Password:_____

Notes:_____

_____

_____

Date:_____

Website:_____

Username:_____

Password:_____

Notes:_____

_____

_____

Date:_____

Website:_____

Username:_____

Password:_____

Notes:_____

_____

_____

Date:_____

Website:_____

Username:_____

Password:_____

Notes:_____

_____

_____

Date:_____

Website:_____

Username:_____

Password:_____

Notes:_____

_____

_____

Date:_____

Website:_____

Username:_____

Password:_____

Notes:_____

_____

_____

Date:_____

Website:_____

Username:_____

Password:_____

Notes:_____

_____

_____

Date:_____

Website:_____

Username:_____

Password:_____

Notes:_____

_____

_____

Date:_____

Website:_____

Username:_____

Password:_____

Notes:_____

_____

_____

Date:_____

Website:_____

Username:_____

Password:_____

Notes:_____

_____

_____

Date:_____

Website:_____

Username:_____

Password:_____

Notes:_____

_____

_____

Date:_____

Website:_____

Username:_____

Password:_____

Notes:_____

_____

_____

Date:_____

Website:_____

Username:_____

Password:_____

Notes:_____

_____

_____

Date:_____

Website:_____

Username:_____

Password:_____

Notes:_____

_____

_____

Date:_____

Website:_____

Username:_____

Password:_____

Notes:_____

_____

_____

Date:_____

Website:_____

Username:_____

Password:_____

Notes:_____

_____

_____

Date:_____

Website:_____

Username:_____

Password:_____

Notes:_____

_____

_____

Date:_____

Website:_____

Username:_____

Password:_____

Notes:_____

_____

_____

Date:_____

Website:_____

Username:_____

Password:_____

Notes:_____

_____

_____

Date:_____

Website:_____

Username:_____

Password:_____

Notes:_____

_____

_____

Date:_____

Website:_____

Username:_____

Password:_____

Notes:_____

_____

_____

Date:_____

Website:_____

Username:_____

Password:_____

Notes:_____

_____

_____

Date:_____

Website:_____

Username:_____

Password:_____

Notes:_____

_____

_____

Date:_____

Website:_____

Username:_____

Password:_____

Notes:_____

_____

_____

Date:_____

Website:_____

Username:_____

Password:_____

Notes:_____

_____

_____

Date:_____

Website:_____

Username:_____

Password:_____

Notes:_____

_____

_____

Date:_____

Website:_____

Username:_____

Password:_____

Notes:_____

_____

_____

Date:_____

Website:_____

Username:_____

Password:_____

Notes:_____

_____

_____

Date:_____

Website:_____

Username:_____

Password:_____

Notes:_____

_____

_____

Date:_____

Website:_____

Username:_____

Password:_____

Notes:_____

_____

_____

Date:_____

Website:_____

Username:_____

Password:_____

Notes:_____

_____

_____

Date:_____

Website:_____

Username:_____

Password:_____

Notes:_____

_____

_____

Date:_____

Website:_____

Username:_____

Password:_____

Notes:_____

_____

_____

Date:_____

Website:_____

Username:_____

Password:_____

Notes:_____

_____

_____

Date:_____

Website:_____

Username:_____

Password:_____

Notes:_____

_____

_____

Date:_____

Website:_____

Username:_____

Password:_____

Notes:_____

_____

_____

Date:_____

Website:_____

Username:_____

Password:_____

Notes:_____

_____

_____

Date:_____

Website:_____

Username:_____

Password:_____

Notes:_____

_____

_____

Date:_____

Website:_____

Username:_____

Password:_____

Notes:_____

_____

_____

Date:_____

Website:_____

Username:_____

Password:_____

Notes:_____

_____

_____

Date:_____

Website:_____

Username:_____

Password:_____

Notes:_____

_____

_____

Date:_____

Website:_____

Username:_____

Password:_____

Notes:_____

_____

_____

Date:_____

Website:_____

Username:_____

Password:_____

Notes:_____

_____

_____

Date:_____

Website:_____

Username:_____

Password:_____

Notes:_____

_____

_____

Date:_____

Website:_____

Username:_____

Password:_____

Notes:_____

_____

_____

Date:_____

Website:_____

Username:_____

Password:_____

Notes:_____

_____

_____

Date:_____

Website:_____

Username:_____

Password:_____

Notes:_____

_____

_____

Date:_____

Website:_____

Username:_____

Password:_____

Notes:_____

_____

_____

Date:_____

Website:_____

Username:_____

Password:_____

Notes:_____

_____

_____

Date:_____

Website:_____

Username:_____

Password:_____

Notes:_____

_____

_____

Date:_____

Website:_____

Username:_____

Password:_____

Notes:_____

_____

_____

Date:_____

Website:_____

Username:_____

Password:_____

Notes:_____

_____

_____

Date:_____

Website:_____

Username:_____

Password:_____

Notes:_____

_____

_____

Date:_____

Website:_____

Username:_____

Password:_____

Notes:_____

_____

_____

Date:_____

Website:_____

Username:_____

Password:_____

Notes:_____

_____

_____

Date:_____

Website:_____

Username:_____

Password:_____

Notes:_____

_____

_____

Date:_____

Website:_____

Username:_____

Password:_____

Notes:_____

_____

_____

Date:_____

Website:_____

Username:_____

Password:_____

Notes:_____

_____

_____

Date:_____

Website:_____

Username:_____

Password:_____

Notes:_____

_____

_____

Date:_____

Website:_____

Username:_____

Password:_____

Notes:_____

_____

_____

Date:_____

Website:_____

Username:_____

Password:_____

Notes:_____

_____

_____

Date:_____

Website:_____

Username:_____

Password:_____

Notes:_____

_____

_____

Date:_____

Website:_____

Username:_____

Password:_____

Notes:_____

_____

_____

Date:_____

Website:_____

Username:_____

Password:_____

Notes:_____

_____

_____

Date:_____

Website:_____

Username:_____

Password:_____

Notes:_____

_____

_____

Date:_____

Website:_____

Username:_____

Password:_____

Notes:_____

_____

_____

Date:_____

Website:_____

Username:_____

Password:_____

Notes:_____

_____

_____

Date:_____

Website:_____

Username:_____

Password:_____

Notes:_____

_____

_____

Date:_____

Website:_____

Username:_____

Password:_____

Notes:_____

_____

_____

Date:_____

Website:_____

Username:_____

Password:_____

Notes:_____

_____

_____

Date:_____

Website:_____

Username:_____

Password:_____

Notes:_____

_____

_____

Date:_____

Website:_____

Username:_____

Password:_____

Notes:_____

_____

_____

Date:_____

Website:_____

Username:_____

Password:_____

Notes:_____

_____

_____

Date:_____

Website:_____

Username:_____

Password:_____

Notes:_____

_____

_____

Date:_____

Website:_____

Username:_____

Password:_____

Notes:_____

_____

_____

Date:_____

Website:_____

Username:_____

Password:_____

Notes:_____

_____

_____

Date:_____

Website:_____

Username:_____

Password:_____

Notes:_____

_____

_____

Date:_____

Website:_____

Username:_____

Password:_____

Notes:_____

_____

_____

Date:_____

Website:_____

Username:_____

Password:_____

Notes:_____

_____

_____

Date:_____

Website:_____

Username:_____

Password:_____

Notes:_____

_____

_____

Date:_____

Website:_____

Username:_____

Password:_____

Notes:_____

_____

_____

Date:_____

Website:_____

Username:_____

Password:_____

Notes:_____

_____

_____

Date:_____

Website:_____

Username:_____

Password:_____

Notes:_____

_____

_____

Date:_____

Website:_____

Username:_____

Password:_____

Notes:_____

_____

_____

Date:_____

Website:_____

Username:_____

Password:_____

Notes:_____

_____

_____

Date:_____

Website:_____

Username:_____

Password:_____

Notes:_____

_____

_____

Date:_____

Website:_____

Username:_____

Password:_____

Notes:_____

_____

_____

Date:_____

Website:_____

Username:_____

Password:_____

Notes:_____

_____

_____

Date:_____

Website:_____

Username:_____

Password:_____

Notes:_____

_____

_____

Date:_____

Website:_____

Username:_____

Password:_____

Notes:_____

_____

_____

Date:_____

Website:_____

Username:_____

Password:_____

Notes:_____

_____

_____

Date:_____

Website:_____

Username:_____

Password:_____

Notes:_____

_____

_____

Date:_____

Website:_____

Username:_____

Password:_____

Notes:_____

_____

_____

Date:_____

Website:_____

Username:_____

Password:_____

Notes:_____

_____

_____

Date:_____

Website:_____

Username:_____

Password:_____

Notes:_____

_____

_____

Date:_____

Website:_____

Username:_____

Password:_____

Notes:_____

_____

_____

Date:_____

Website:_____

Username:_____

Password:_____

Notes:_____

_____

_____

Date:_____

Website:_____

Username:_____

Password:_____

Notes:_____

_____

_____

Date:_____

Website:_____

Username:_____

Password:_____

Notes:_____

_____

_____

Date:_____

Website:_____

Username:_____

Password:_____

Notes:_____

_____

_____

Date:_____

Website:_____

Username:_____

Password:_____

Notes:_____

_____

_____

Date:_____

Website:_____

Username:_____

Password:_____

Notes:_____

_____

_____

Date:_____

Website:_____

Username:_____

Password:_____

Notes:_____

_____

_____

Date:_____

Website:_____

Username:_____

Password:_____

Notes:_____

_____

_____

Date:_____

Website:_____

Username:_____

Password:_____

Notes:_____

_____

_____

Date:_____

Website:_____

Username:_____

Password:_____

Notes:_____

_____

_____

Date:_____

Website:_____

Username:_____

Password:_____

Notes:_____

_____

_____

Date:_____

Website:_____

Username:_____

Password:_____

Notes:_____

_____

_____

Date:_____

Website:_____

Username:_____

Password:_____

Notes:_____

_____

_____

Date:_____

Website:_____

Username:_____

Password:_____

Notes:_____

_____

_____

Date:_____

Website:_____

Username:_____

Password:_____

Notes:_____

_____

_____

Date:_____

Website:_____

Username:_____

Password:_____

Notes:_____

_____

_____

Date:_____

Website:_____

Username:_____

Password:_____

Notes:_____

_____

_____

Date:_____

Website:_____

Username:_____

Password:_____

Notes:_____

_____

_____

Date:_____

Website:_____

Username:_____

Password:_____

Notes:_____

_____

_____

www.ingramcontent.com/pod-product-compliance
Lightning Source LLC
Chambersburg PA
CBHW051113050326
40690CB00006B/775